We the People

The My Lai Massacre

by Michael Burgan

Content Adviser: David L. Anderson, Ph.D.,
Professor of History,
California State University, Monterey Bay

Reading Adviser: Rosemary Palmer, Ph.D.,
Department of Literacy, College of Education,
Boise State University

Compass Point Books · Minneapolis, Minnesota

Compass Point Books
151 Good Counsel Drive
P.O. Box 669
Mankato, MN 56002-0669

Printed in the United States of America.

 This book was manufactured with paper containing at least 10 percent post-consumer waste.

On the cover: U.S. soldier stokes a house fire during the My Lai massacre.

Photographs ©: Time & Life Pictures/Getty Images, cover, 4, 6, 14, 19, 21, 22, 29, 33, 37, 38; Prints Old & Rare, back cover (far left); Library of Congress, back cover, 12; Getty Images, 9, 11; AP Images, 5, 17, 24, 25, 27, 30, 31, 40; Bettmann/Corbis, 35.

Editor: Julie Gassman
Page Production: Bobbie Nuytten
Photo Researcher: Robert McConnell
Cartographer: XNR Productions, Inc.
Library Consultant: Kathleen Baxter

Art Director: LuAnn Ascheman-Adams
Creative Director: Keith Griffin
Editorial Director: Nick Healy
Managing Editor: Catherine Neitge

Library of Congress Cataloging-in-Publication Data
Burgan, Michael.
My Lai massacre / by Michael Burgan.
p. cm. — (We the people)
Includes index.
ISBN 978-0-7565-3849-1 (library binding)
1. My Lai Massacre, Vietnam, 1968—Juvenile literature. I. Title. II. Series.
DS557.8.M9B87 2008
959.704'3—dc22 2008006286

Visit Compass Point Books on the Internet at *www.compasspointbooks.com*
or e-mail your request to *custserv@compasspointbooks.com*

The My Lai Massacre • The My Lai Massacre • The My Lai Massacre

Table of Contents

A Bloody Day

In the sky, helicopter propellers cut through the air. The copters carried a platoon of U.S. Army soldiers to the small village of My Lai, South Vietnam. It was March 1968, and the men were part of a larger army. In all, more than 500,000 U.S. troops were fighting in the Vietnam War.

About 100 soldiers were sent on the My Lai mission.

The United States was battling South Vietnamese forces called the Viet Cong (VC). The Viet Cong were fighting against the government of South Vietnam. They received help from North Vietnam, which wanted to take over South Vietnam and become one country. The Viet Cong were guerrillas—soldiers who travel in small groups, take the enemy by surprise, and then run away. They dressed like civilians and often lived with them. U.S. troops could never be sure whether the South Vietnamese they saw were friendly civilians or dangerous Viet Cong.

Lieutenant William Calley Jr.

A 24-year-old lieutenant named William Calley Jr. led the platoon that arrived first in My Lai. Calley and his men came to

My Lai to destroy a VC base nearby. As the American soldiers left the helicopters, they began firing their weapons toward the village. They expected the enemy to be near. But the VC had already fled the area. The only people who remained in My Lai were women, children, and the elderly.

Over the next few hours, gunfire and bloodshed filled My Lai. Calley and other platoon members later claimed they had orders to kill the unarmed civilians.

The bodies of murdered civilians lay where they fell after being shot.

About the War

The Vietnam War was fought from 1959 to 1975. South Vietnam battled the communist Viet Cong of the South and the communists of North Vietnam. (Communists believe in an economic system in which goods and property are owned by the government and shared in common. Communist rulers limit personal freedoms to achieve their goals.)

The Viet Cong and the North Vietnamese wanted to unite the two countries into one communist nation. They were backed by the Soviet Union and China. The United States supported the South Vietnamese with money and troops. The first American combat troops arrived in 1965. By 1967, there were more than 500,000 U.S. troops fighting in Vietnam.

The fighting grew costly in lives and money. Protests against the war increased. In 1973, a cease-fire agreement was reached, and U.S. troops were withdrawn. Fighting continued, however, until 1975, when the North took control of a united Vietnam.

The war killed more than 58,000 Americans and between 2 million and 4 million Vietnamese. More than 300,000 Americans were wounded during the war, the longest in U.S. history. The effects of the long, bloody war are still felt today.

The officers above Calley said they had not given that order. Calley and some of his men killed several hundred civilians on that day, March 16, 1968. The events came to be known as the My Lai Massacre.

Those involved in the killings tried to keep the massacre a secret. But slowly Army commanders began learning what had happened at My Lai. More than a year passed before the rest of the world heard the truth about the massacre. Calley and several other soldiers faced a military trial called a court-martial for their roles in the killings. By then, millions of Americans opposed U.S. involvement in the Vietnam War. The My Lai Massacre deepened their belief that the United States should leave South Vietnam.

A Full-Scale War

The United States became involved in the battle between North and South Vietnam in an attempt to keep communism from spreading. Initially the United States only provided South Vietnam with military supplies and

U.S. troops helped deliver supplies to South Vietnamese soldiers.

training. But by 1965, U.S. President Lyndon B. Johnson wanted to increase efforts to fight the communists in Vietnam. He ordered U.S. planes to bomb North Vietnam and sent the first U.S. combat troops to South Vietnam. By the end of the year, 184,000 American troops were stationed there. The North Vietnamese also sent their soldiers to the south, to help the Viet Cong battle the Americans.

Although the United States had a more powerful army, it faced many difficulties in South Vietnam. Much of the country was covered with thick jungle, where the Viet Cong could easily hide. The weather there was often hot and humid, with temperatures soaring above 100 degrees Fahrenheit (38 degrees Celsius). Other times, heavy rains fell. Soldiers had trouble keeping their equipment dry, and they battled ailments such as malaria and skin disease. Writer Philip Caputo, who served in Vietnam, wrote, "The sun scorched us in the dry season, and in the [rainy] season we were pounded numb by ceaseless rain."

Perhaps the greatest problem for the Americans was

Soldiers often had to wade through waist-high water while moving through the jungle.

identifying who were friends and who were enemies. The Viet Cong often lived with the residents of small villages. They fled the towns when the Americans neared, then

American military advisers sat with a Vietnamese woman and children after their village was destroyed because U.S. troops thought it was a Viet Cong stronghold.

returned later. Some South Vietnamese supported the Viet Cong in their war, so they helped the guerrillas. Others feared they would be killed if they did not actively support the Viet Cong or at least refuse to help the Americans.

Writer Tim O'Brien was a U.S. soldier in the area

around My Lai. He said some South Vietnamese would not answer questions about the Viet Cong. The Americans did not know whether the VC were near "until we ducked [one's] bullet or stepped on his land mine," O'Brien said.

The villagers sometimes hid weapons for the guerrillas, and women were known to fight for the VC. The Americans feared that the women they saw in the villages—and even the children—might try to attack them. Because of this civilian aid, many U.S. soldiers distrusted and feared any South Vietnamese they met.

Charlie Company Goes to War

On December 1, 1967, a group of about 125 U.S. soldiers called Charlie Company reached South Vietnam. They were part of a larger force called Task Force Barker. Their goal was to search out Viet Cong bases and destroy them.

Villages like Ben Suc, which was destroyed by Americans, served as Viet Cong supply centers and meeting places.

They also moved civilians who were considered friendly to the Viet Cong to camps where they could be watched.

At the end of January 1968, North Vietnam launched the Tet Offensive, a series of major attacks on South Vietnamese cities. The U.S. and South Vietnamese forces drove back the attacks. The men of Charlie Company heard fighting near their base, which was about 350 miles (560 kilometers) northeast of Saigon. Soon they were sent to locate retreating enemy troops.

Many of the VC entered a region the Americans called Pinkville, because it was colored pink on their maps. One of the villages there was called Son My, and within it was an even smaller village called My Lai.

Charlie Company had three platoons. The officer in charge of the First Platoon was Lieutenant William Calley. Starting in February, he and his men had done their first real fighting in South Vietnam. They had seen their friends die from enemy rifle fire and mines. After seeing death up close, Calley later said, he finally realized "that we weren't

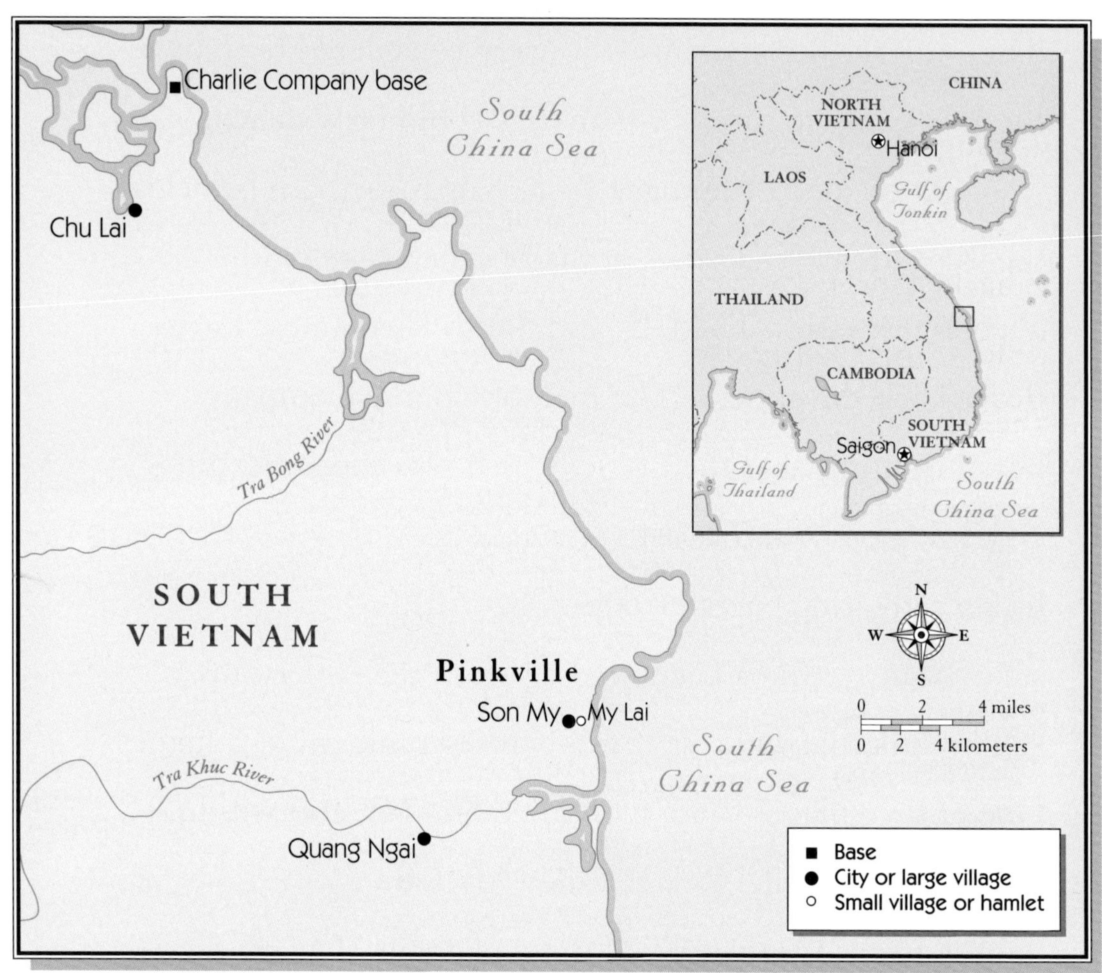

Charlie Company's base was northwest of My Lai.

playing games." He and some other men in the company began to feel intense hatred for all the Vietnamese they saw. Their commander, Captain Ernest Medina, seemed to share some of these feelings. The men of Charlie Company began to beat some prisoners. They forced others to lead the way through fields thought to have land mines buried in them.

On Thursday, March 14, a mine killed a member of Charlie Company's Third Platoon. The next day, the men held a funeral. Following the ceremony, Medina discussed the next mission. Charlie Company would go by helicopter

Captain Medina had served as Charlie Company's commanding officer for about two years before the massacre at My Lai.

to the village of My Lai. About 250 Viet Cong were thought to be staying there, and the civilians there actively supported the VC. Medina told his men, "The village could be destroyed … burn the houses down, kill all livestock … cut any of the crops that might feed the VC."

A soldier asked what they should do about civilians. Medina later claimed he had said they should only attack civilians who seemed a threat. But about 20 soldiers, including Calley, later said the captain told them to kill anyone in the village.

Calley gave his men a separate talk, telling them to expect to meet many armed men, with women helping them. What many of the men heard—or thought they heard—from their officers became mixed with their own hatred for the Vietnamese. Those thoughts and feelings fueled what happened the next day.

The Massacre

On March 16, 1968, just before 7:30 A.M., U.S. artillery began to fire on My Lai. The guns were located outside the village in a well-protected spot. The gunners were trying to

The soldiers approached the village with their weapons ready.

wipe out any enemy that might be waiting to attack Charlie Company's helicopters. The helicopters landed safely, and Calley's men hit the ground first and began firing into the village with guns, rockets, and grenades. They soon realized that the enemy was not firing back. Medina and the officers above him had been wrong—there were no Viet Cong in My Lai. Still, the men of Charlie Company had a mission to destroy the village, and they went to work.

The men in each platoon split up into smaller groups. Most fired automatic rifles, which could fire 30 bullets in just 2.4 seconds. As they went through My Lai, the soldiers killed the animals of the village. People who ran away from the troops were shot. Some of the troops tried to order the Vietnamese out of their homes. But the Americans spoke little Vietnamese, and the residents of My Lai did not speak English, creating confusion. Some soldiers did not even try to talk to the villagers or take them prisoner. The Americans threw grenades into their straw homes and the bunkers where the residents hid during battles.

A soldier stoked the fire of burning houses in the village.

As the morning went on, the attacks on civilians grew worse. Some of the soldiers sexually abused the Vietnamese women before killing them. Children and babies were killed, too. Private Butch Gruver later reported seeing a wounded boy who was 3 or 4, watching the assault. "He just stood there with big eyes staring like he didn't believe

A group of women and children stood terrified, knowing they would be killed.

what was happening." A radio operator then shot the boy.

At the center of the massacre was Lieutenant Calley. When a large group of prisoners was rounded up, he ordered two soldiers to "take care of them." The men thought he meant guard the Vietnamese. Instead, he told them, "Come on, we'll line them up; we'll kill them." The two soldiers began firing, but one of them, Paul Meadlo, stopped. Tears filled his eyes—he could not stand the thought of killing more women and children. Calley then began firing into the crowd. Later Calley ordered the killing of another group of civilians, and once again he fired at the Vietnamese.

Not all the soldiers took part in the massacre. Thomas Partsch did not fire his gun, and one sergeant ordered his men to fire only if someone fired at them. Several of the men also tried to help children wounded in the shooting. Hugh Thompson, a helicopter pilot, landed at the scene. He was shocked to hear soldiers say they were killing civilians. He threatened to fire on the Americans if they did not stop their killing. Thompson then arranged for another helicopter to take away some of the Vietnamese, and he and his crew brought a young boy to a hospital. But many of the soldiers kept killing unarmed civilians. Finally, around 10:30 A.M., the shooting stopped.

The World Learns About My Lai

During the morning, Captain Medina came to the battle scene. He later claimed he ordered the killing to stop when he saw it. Some of his men, however, say he ignored the killing of civilians and even ordered some to be killed.

The officers above Medina also had some idea of the massacre. They flew in helicopters over the village and saw the bodies of dead civilians. They also received reports about civilian deaths.

Major General Samuel Koster, who was in charge of the Army's largest division in Vietnam, flew over My Lai the morning of the massacre.

Several hours after the massacre,

Medina received an order from his commander, Lieutenant Colonel Frank Barker. He wanted Medina to go back to My Lai and learn how many people were killed. Major General Samuel Koster, however, outranked Barker. He accepted Medina's first report that about 25 civilians had been killed, all by artillery. Koster told Medina to ignore Barker's order to return to My Lai.

By this time, pilot Hugh Thompson had already tried to expose what happened at My Lai. He had returned to his base around noon and told his commanding officer about the killing he saw. Thompson's report reached a general in Vietnam, but the general and other officers on the ground did not want to fully investigate the

Warrant Officer Hugh Thompson

events at My Lai. Killing unarmed civilians is a crime. The officers did not want officials in Washington, D.C., to think they had ordered the attack or could not control their men.

In all, about 30 officers learned of the massacre. The people who knew about My Lai tried to hide it from the rest of the Army—and the world. They did not look further into what had happened or try to punish anyone involved. Still, reports of the My Lai Massacre did leak out. In April 1968, Private Gruver told a soldier named Ronald Ridenhour what happened. Gruver guessed that up to 400 civilians were killed that day. He also noted that one American shot himself in the foot so he would not have to take part in the massacre.

During the following year, Ridenhour talked to other members of Charlie Company. Some were upset by what they had seen or done that day, and they gladly gave him more details about the attack. One soldier said Captain Medina warned him not to "do anything stupid like write my congressman." That soldier obeyed Medina, but

Ridenhour decided he had to write to members of Congress and tell them what happened at My Lai.

In his letter of March 29, 1969, he described everything he had learned from Gruver and the others. He told them the men believed that Medina wanted Charlie

After the war, Ronald Ridenhour became a respected journalist.

The My Lai Massacre • The My Lai Massacre • The My Lai

Company to kill all the civilians and that Lieutenant Calley had killed two large groups of Vietnamese. Ridenhour then added, "Exactly what did, in fact, occur … I do not know for certain, but I am convinced that it was something very black [evil] indeed."

After reading Ridenhour's letter, several members of Congress asked U.S. Army officials in Washington, D.C., about what happened at My Lai. Of course, the officials could not find any reports of a large number of civilian deaths at My Lai or investigations into such claims. However, the Army now began to take a closer look at Charlie Company and its actions on March 16, 1968.

The officials in Washington soon learned that the claims of a massacre were true. They also dicovered that officers above Captain Medina had tried to hide the truth. One of the men who helped uncover the facts was Hugh Thompson. He identified Calley as one of the men he had seen firing into a crowd of civilians. Later, Private First Class Paul Meadlo described how Calley ordered him to kill civilians. In September 1969, the Army began to collect information to see whether it should charge Calley with a crime. Finally, that November, he was arrested and charged with killing more than 100 civilians at My Lai.

While the Army was preparing to arrest and charge Calley, a reporter named Seymour Hersh heard rumors about My Lai. Throughout the Vietnam War, U.S. officials did not always share the truth about the military's actions in Vietnam. So reporters such as Hersh tried to learn the truth about the fighting.

Paul Meadlo, who refused to shoot civilians at My Lai, later testified against William Calley.

Seymour Hersh

After hearing the rumors, Hersh talked to Ridenhour, Calley, and some of the soldiers who had been in Pinkville in March 1968. In a series of articles published in November, the reporter described the killings. His stories appeared in 35 newspapers across the country.

Pictures taken at the massacre appeared in *The Plain Dealer*, a Cleveland newspaper. Later they appeared in *Life*, a popular weekly magazine, and news about My Lai was broadcast on television. The whole world now knew about Calley and My Lai. Some Americans were shocked to learn that American soldiers could kill women and children, even during a difficult war.

The Trial

At the end of November 1969, the Army began a huge investigation into the My Lai Massacre. Lieutenant General William R. Peers and other officers formed the Peers Commission. Its members were given the task of questioning soldiers who had been there and the officers who had given orders to Charlie Company. Their final report was called the Peers Report. It found that the massacre had indeed taken place. It

Known for his fairness, Lieutenant General William R. Peers worked at least six days a week for four months to uncover the truth about My Lai.

said that by covering up the deaths of all but between 20 and 28 civilians, the officers hid a much greater war crime. The commission, however, did not learn something that Seymour Hersh discovered later: U.S. officers in South Vietnam destroyed papers describing the massacre.

The Peers Commission decided that U.S. officers in Vietnam had hidden the truth about My Lai. Now Calley and several other men would face a military trial to decide whether they were guilty of war crimes. Of the men, Calley's name had appeared most often in newspapers and on TV, and his court-martial became one of the most famous in U.S. history.

Many Americans, however, did not think Calley should face a court-martial. They considered him a scapegoat—someone chosen to take all the blame for the actions of others. These Americans thought Calley was a good soldier trying to do the best he could in a dangerous situation. They respected his decision to serve in the Army at a time when many young Americans were trying to get out

Members of an American Legion post in Georgia raised money and gathered petition signatures in support of William Calley.

of joining the military. Calley received up to 5,000 letters a week, most coming from Americans who thought he was innocent. They thought he had simply done what many other soldiers had done before when faced with possible enemy forces.

Calley's trial began on November 17, 1970, at Fort Benning, Georgia. Soldiers who had served under him described the killings at My Lai and how Calley ordered several of them to fire at unarmed civilians. Paul Meadlo said Calley himself fired hundreds of bullets at My Lai villagers huddled in a ditch.

Calley told the court that Captain Medina had ordered him to kill the civilians. He said, "I felt then—and I still do—that I acted as directed, I carried out my orders, and I did not feel wrong in doing so." Medina, however, denied giving Calley that order.

In the end, the jury believed the evidence against Calley. On March 29, 1971, they found Calley guilty of killing 22 South Vietnamese. He was sentenced to life in prison, but later the punishment was reduced to 20 years. In a separate trial, Captain Medina was found not guilty. The jurors believed his account of what happened that day.

Following the verdict, Calley was escorted to the Fort Benning stockade to begin his prison term.

He said he had not known about the killing until late in the attack and that he had ordered it to stop as soon as he saw what was happening.

After the Trial

The Vietnam War sharply divided Americans. Starting in 1965, thousands of college students protested the war. Still, opinion polls that year found that about 80 percent of Americans supported the U.S. role in the war. Over time, however, support for the war faded, as tens of thousands of Americans died in the fighting. Several months after the Tet Offensive of January 1968, more than half of Americans thought it had been a mistake to send U.S. troops to Vietnam.

Antiwar protests grew larger, and by the time of Calley's trial, even more Americans wanted the war to end. Others, however, believed the United States had to defeat communist forces in South Vietnam, or else it and more countries in the region would become communist.

The Calley trial and verdict seemed to unite many people on both sides of the issue. As many as 78 percent of the people polled disagreed with the verdict. Another poll showed that just over half of Americans wanted

President Richard Nixon to use his powers to free Calley or at least reduce his sentence. Many members of Congress also defended Calley.

In general, the Americans who opposed the Vietnam War thought it was wrong to blame Calley. Focusing on him as the scapegoat took attention away from officers and government officials who had made mistakes throughout the war and tried to cover up the massacre. People who supported the war

Supporters of the war held demonstrations against antiwar activists.

William Calley's role in the My Lai Massacre was the cover story of Time's *December 5, 1969, issue.*

tended to see Calley as a good soldier. They thought the troops in Vietnam faced a dangerous enemy, and they had to be able to defend themselves.

A few newspapers reported before the trial that some Americans did not even believe the massacre had happened. One officer on the jury, however, said he thought Calley's supporters were swept up by their emotions and were ignoring the facts. He said Calley had brutally killed innocent women and children—"a rather harsh treatment, and a rather final treatment."

Even as Calley was on trial, U.S. troops were coming home from Vietnam. President Nixon wanted to slowly end the U.S. presence there and let South Vietnam do more of the fighting. Most American troops were out of South Vietnam by the end of 1973, and the war ended with North Vietnam's victory in 1975. But Americans still argued over whether the country should have gone to war in the first place or stayed in Vietnam so long.

After several appeals, President Nixon commuted

The last major group of Americans to leave Vietnam arrived in the United States in late March 1973.

Calley's sentence, and he was released from prison in November 1974. He hoped to win a new trial so he could try again to prove his innocence, but two U.S. courts said no. Calley then married and moved to Georgia, where he spent many years working in a jewelry store and tried to put his crimes behind him.

As the years passed, most Americans forgot the details of the My Lai Massacre. But in 2003, the United States went to war in Iraq. Once again, U.S. troops faced an enemy that lived among civilians. Soon reports of a few soldiers' killing innocent Iraqis emerged. While these reports were investigated, some Americans were upset to think their soldiers could act so cruelly. Others were reminded of the My Lai Massacre and the horrible incidents that can occur in any war.

Glossary

artillery—large weapons, such as cannons or missile launchers, that require several soldiers to load, aim, and fire

bunkers—holes in the ground where people seek shelter during attacks

civilians—people who are not in the military

commuted—changed a penalty to another one that is less severe

congressman—person elected to serve in Congress, the lawmaking branch of the U.S. government

court-martial—trial for members of the military accused of breaking rules or committing a crime

grenades—small explosives that can be thrown

guerrillas—soldiers who are not part of a country's regular army; guerrillas often use surprise attacks against an enemy

land mine—explosive device buried just below ground

massacre—killing of a large number of helpless people

platoon—military unit ranging in size from 30 to 50 soldiers

Did You Know?

- A song written about William Calley was recorded while he was on trial. "The Battle Hymn of Lt. Calley" was sung to the tune of "The Battle Hymn of the Republic" and defended Calley. The song sold 200,000 copies in just a few days.

- Task Force Barker, of which Charlie Company was a part, was named for Lieutenant Colonel Frank Barker. His exact role in giving the order to destroy My Lai and cover up the massacre was never known. Barker died in a helicopter crash several months after the massacre.

- The official U.S. name for My Lai was "My Lai (4)." Five other villages in the area had the same name, with different numbers. The residents of My Lai (4) called their village Tu Cung.

- U.S. Army officers at the School of Advanced Military Studies at Fort Leavenworth, Kansas, still study the My Lai Massacre to learn from the mistakes made by William Calley and others.

IMPORTANT DATES

Timeline

1967 Lieutenant William Calley Jr. and Charlie Company arrive in South Vietnam.

1968 On March 14, a member of Charlie Company is killed by an enemy explosion; two days later, Charlie Company destroys the village of My Lai.

1969 In late March, Ronald Ridenhour tells members of Congress about the My Lai Massacre; in November, Seymour Hersh publishes the first detailed reports of the massacre.

1970 In November, the court-martial of William Calley begins in November.

1971 On March 29, Calley is found guilty of killing 22 South Vietnamese civilians.

1974 In November, Calley is released from prison.

Important People

William Calley Jr. (1943–)

U.S. Army lieutenant sent to prison for his role in the killings at My Lai; he joined the Army in 1966 and trained in Georgia to become an officer; his life sentence was reduced to 20 years, but he was released from prison in November 1974 and paroled, meaning his sentence was over

Seymour Hersh (1937–)

Journalist who wrote about the My Lai Massacre and Army efforts to hide the massacre from the public; his work earned him a Pulitzer Prize, the highest award for U.S. journalists; in later years, Hersh investigated the torture of Iraqi prisoners by Americans during the Iraq war

Ernest Medina (1936–)

Captain who ordered Charlie Company to destroy My Lai; claimed he did not tell the soldiers to kill civilians; Medina was charged with murder because he knew about the killings but did not try to stop them; he was found not guilty and left the Army

Hugh Thompson (1943–2006)

One of the heroes of the My Lai Massacre; he landed his helicopter to rescue some of the civilians at My Lai; later he gave details of the massacre to the Peers Commission; he was shunned by fellow soldiers for years, but eventually given the Soldier's Medal for his actions

WANT TO KNOW MORE?

More Books to Read

Burgan, Michael. *Lyndon Baines Johnson*. Minneapolis: Compass Point Books, 2004.

Caputo, Philip. *Ten Thousand Days of Thunder: A History of the Vietnam War*. New York: Atheneum Books for Young Readers, 2005.

Galt, Margot Fortunato. *Stop This War! American Protest of the Conflict in Vietnam*. Minneapolis: Lerner Publications, 2000.

Gibson, Karen Bush. *The Vietnam War*. Hockessin, Del.: Mitchell Lane Publishers, 2007.

Harrison, Paul. *The Cold War*. San Diego: Lucent Books, 2005.

On the Web

For more information on this topic, use FactHound.

1. Go to *www.facthound.com*
2. Type in this book ID: 0756538491
3. Click on the *Fetch It* button.

FactHound will find the best Web sites for you.

On the Road

Vietnam Veterans Memorial
National Mall
Washington, DC
202/426-6841
National monument that honors troops killed or missing in Vietnam; Vietnam Women's Memorial is nearby

Vietnam War Museum
954 W. Carmen Ave.
Chicago, IL 60640
773/728-6111
Located in the city's Little Saigon area, the museum features uniforms and gear from the Vietnam War

Look for more We the People books about this era:

The 19th Amendment
The Berlin Airlift
The Civil Rights Act of 1964
The Draft Lottery
The Dust Bowl
Ellis Island
The Fall of Saigon
GI Joe in World War II
The Great Depression
The Holocaust Museum
The Kent State Shootings
The Korean War
Navajo Code Talkers
The Negro Leagues
Pearl Harbor
The Persian Gulf War
The San Francisco Earthquake of 1906
Selma's Bloody Sunday
September 11
The Sinking of the USS Indianapolis
The Statue of Liberty
The Tet Offensive
The Titanic
The Tuskegee Airmen
Vietnam Veterans Memorial
Vietnam War POWs

A complete list of We the People titles is available on our Web site: www.compasspointbooks.com

Index

About the Author

Michael Burgan is a freelance writer of books for children and adults. A history graduate of the University of Connecticut, he has written more than 100 fiction and nonfiction children's books. For adult audiences, he has written news articles, essays, and plays. Burgan is a recipient of an Educational Press Association of America award.